LESLEY ANNE IVORY'S
COLLECTABLE CATS

Chronicle Books · San Francisco

I hesitate a little to speak of his capacity for friendship and the affectionateness of his nature, for I know from his own reserve that he would not care to have it much talked about. We understood each other perfectly, but we never made any fuss about it; when I spoke his name and snapped my fingers, he came to me; when I returned home at night, he was pretty sure to be waiting for me near the gate, and would rise and saunter along the walk, as if his being there was purely accidental – so shy was he commonly of showing feeling. There was one thing he never did – he never rushed through an open doorway. He never forgot his dignity. If he had asked to have the door opened, and was eager to go out, he always went out deliberately; I can see him now, standing on the sill, looking about at the sky as if he was thinking whether it were worth while to take an umbrella, until he was near having his tail shut in.

CHARLES DUDLEY WARNER, *MY SUMMER IN A GARDEN*

Anyone who has lived on terms of comparative equality with a cat knows that he will show his intelligence fifty times a day. To be sure this intelligence is usually of the variety called selfish. Thereby the cat shows how much finer his intelligence is than that of the rest of the animal world. He is quite unwilling to perform feats of intelligence for which he can see no legitimate reason, or through which he is unable to derive any personal satisfaction. If he wants submaxillary massage he knows that he is pretty sure of getting it by leaping into someone's lap. If he does not want it he knows that the best way of avoiding it is to avoid the person who insists on lavishing it. A cat, it has been said, will only come when called if dinner is in the offing. This is very much my procedure. I refuse to make casual calls but often accept invitations to dinner.

CARL VAN VECHTEN, *THE TIGER IN THE HOUSE*

She was the most motherly thing I have ever known. She was never happy without a family. Indeed, I cannot remember her when she hadn't a family in one stage or another. She was not very particular about what sort of family it was. If she could not have kittens, then she would content herself with puppies or rats. Anything that she could wash and feed seemed to satisfy her. I believe she would have brought up chickens if we had entrusted them to her.

All her brains must have run to motherliness, for she hadn't much sense. She could never tell the difference between her own children and other people's. She thought anything young was a kitten. We once mixed up a spaniel puppy that had lost its own mother among her progeny. I shall never forget her astonishment when it first barked. She boxed both its ears, and then sat looking down at it with an expression of indignant sorrow that was really touching.

JEROME K. JEROME, *NOVEL NOTES*

They tell me I am beautiful: they praise my silken hair,
  My little feet that silently slip on from stair to stair:
They praise my pretty trustful face and innocent grey eye;
Fond hands caress me oftentimes, yet would that I might die!

Why was I born to be abhorred of man and bird and beast?
The bullfinch marks me stealing by, and straight his song
    hath ceased;
The shrewmouse eyes me shudderingly, then flees; and,
    worse than that,
The housedog he flees after me – why was I born a cat?

CHARLES STUART CALVERLEY, 'SAD MEMORIES'

There is another thing I must mention of a momentous kind; – but I must mind my periods in it – Mrs Dilke has two Cats – a Mother and a Daughter – now the Mother is a tabby and the daughter a black and white like the spotted child – Now it appears ominous to me, for the doors of both houses are opened frequently – so that there is a complete thoroughfare for both Cats (there being no board up to the contrary), they may one and several of them come into my room *ad libitum*. But no – the Tabby only comes – whether from sympathy from Ann the Maid or me I cannot tell . . . The Cat is not an old Maid herself – her daughter is a proof of it. I have questioned her – I have looked at the lines of her paw – I have felt her pulse – to no purpose – Why should the *old* Cat come to me? I ask myself – and myself has not a word to answer. It may come to light some day; if it does you shall hear of it . . .

JOHN KEATS, LETTER TO GEORGE AND GEORGIANA, HIS BROTHER AND SISTER

Come, lovely cat, and rest upon my heart,
    And let my gaze dive in the cold
Live pools of thine enchanted eyes that dart
    Metallic rays of green and gold.

My fascinated hands caress at leisure
    Thy head and supple back, and when
Thy soft electric body fills with pleasure
    My thrilled and drunken fingers, then

Thou changest to my woman; for her glance,
    Like thine, most lovable of creatures,
Is icy, deep, and cleaving as a lance.

    And round her hair and sphinx-like features
And round her dusky form floats, vaguely blent,
    A subtle air and dangerous scent.

CHARLES BAUDELAIRE, 'COME, LOVELY CAT',
FROM *LES FLEURS DU MAL*

The cat invented radar and extrasensory perception long before we ever thought of it. Nobody has ever heard a cat 'miaow' to or at another cat. They shout and yell and scream when preparing for battle, but they don't talk audibly to one another. Their little cries are reserved for us. Yet somehow either through the antennae of their whiskers, or pure thought broadcasters and receivers, they are attuned to one another and know what is going on. And if they can do this, what is to prevent them from penetrating our thoughts – if not now, then eventually? I have always been just a little wary of letting cats know too much about my business, and I have encountered people who when talking before their cat and working on the theory that it cannot spell will say, 'Did you put the l-o-b-s-t-e-r in the f-r-i-d-g-e?'

PAUL GALLICO, *HONOURABLE CAT*

It is odd that cats show an intense dislike to anything destined or set apart for them. Mentu had a basket of his own, and a cushion made by a fond mistress, but to put him into it was to make him bound out like an india-rubber ball. He liked to occupy proper chairs and sofas, or even proper hearthrugs. In the same way, the well-bred cat has an inconvenient but aesthetic preference for eating its food in pleasant places, even as we consume chilly tea and dusty bread and butter in a summer glade. A plate is distasteful to a cat, a newspaper still worse; they like to eat sticky pieces of meat sitting on a cushioned chair or a nice Persian rug. Yet if these were dedicated to this use they would remove elsewhere. Hence the controversy is interminable.

MARGARET BENSON, *THE SOUL OF A CAT*

It is necessary to say that if the cat holds a big place in the household it is not alone by his graces of spoiled child, his loving caresses, and the seductive abandon of his lovely indolence; more than anything it is because he demands so much. His personality is strong, his awakenings and his wishes impatient. He refuses to wait. Under his supple grace his gesture is one of insistence and command. You defend yourself in vain, he is master and you yield.

MADAME MICHELET, *LES CHATS*

When I caught my cat staring, patronizingly
I felt like disturbing her equanimity.
Don't you ever dream of your distant relation
Prowling through tropical forest and plain?
I asked. Wouldn't bigger game bring more elation
Than eyeing suburban cats in the rain?
How would antelope, I winked, compare with what
    you're eating?
How could anything, she blinked, compare with
    central heating?

A narrow outlook, this, it seemed to me –
But how to prove her guilty of complacency?
There must be something, I thought, she would prefer . . .
A big log fire – and I bought a rug for her.
Tonight she narrows her eyes invitingly;
I think she has something to share with me.
The new carpet suits me fine, she says when I inquire,
Oh, and all this area is mine, from here to the fire.

STEPHEN CORBETT, 'A CAT'S GRATITUDE'

See the kitten on the wall
  Sporting with the leaves that fall,
Withered leaves – one – two – and three –
From the lofty elder tree!
– But the kitten, how she starts,
Crouches, stretches, paws, and darts!
First at one, and then its fellow
Just as light and just as yellow.
There are many now – now one –
Now they stop and there are none.

What intenseness of desire
In her upward eye of fire!
With a tiger-leap half way
Now she meets the coming prey,
Lets it go as fast, and then
Has it in her power again.
Now she works with three or four,
Like an Indian conjurer;
Quick as he in feats of art,
Far beyond in joy of heart.

WILLIAM WORDSWORTH, 'THE KITTEN AND FALLING LEAVES'

I'm so white that my whiteness seems merely a kind of lure, a stealthy trick of reflections. When there are leaves above me, I turn green, and blue cinerarias cast upon my flanks a splash of tranquil indigo that barely stirs when I breathe. Have you never seen me rose-coloured at the hour when the great cirrus clouds flee before the setting sun like a flight of flamingoes? It tires me to have all these colours taking possession of me, because my childhood without a nurse has left me delicate and sensitive, very much taken up with my own fragility and the attention it secures for me. I'm pensive as an angel, and if I often close my eyelids it's to prevent the blue of the sky from meeting and deepening the blue of my eyes.

COLETTE, *DIALOGUES DES BETES*

A leaky beer-tap was the cause of her downfall. A saucer used to be placed underneath it to catch the drippings. One day the cat, coming in thirsty, and finding nothing else to drink, lapped up a little, liked it, and lapped a little more . . .

From that day till the hour she died, I don't believe that cat was ever once quite sober. Her days she passed in a drunken stupor before the kitchen fire. Her nights she spent in the beer cellar.

My grandmother, shocked and grieved beyond expression, gave up her barrel and adopted bottles. The cat, thus condemned to enforced abstinence, meandered about the house for a day and a half in a disconsolate, quarrelsome mood. Then she disappeared, returning at eleven o'clock as tight as a drum.

Where she went, and how she managed to procure the drink, we never discovered; but the same programme was repeated every day. Some time during the morning she would contrive to elude our vigilance and escape; and late every evening she would come reeling home across the fields in a condition that I will not sully my pen by attempting to describe.

JEROME K. JEROME, *NOVEL NOTES*

With Richelieu the taste for cats was a mania; when he rose in the morning and when he went to bed at night he was always surrounded by a dozen of them with which he played, delighting to watch them jump and gambol. He had one of his chambers fitted up as a cattery, which was entrusted to overseers, the names of whom are known. Abel and Teyssandier came, morning and evening, to feed the cats with *pâtés* fashioned of the white meat of chicken. At his death Richelieu left a pension for his cats and to Abel and Teyssandier so that they might continue to care for their charges. When he died Richelieu left fourteen cats of which the names were: Mounard le Fougueux, Soumise, Serpolet, Gazette, Ludovic le Cruel, Mimie Piaillon, Felimare, Lucifer, Lodoïska, Rubis sur l'Ongle, Pyrame, Thisbé, Racan, and Perruque. These last two received their names from the fact that they were born in the wig of Racan, the academician.

ALEXANDRE LANDRIN, *LE CHAT*

One evening we were all, except father, going to a ball, and when we started, we left 'the Master' and his cat in the drawing-room together. 'The Master' was reading at a small table; suddenly the candle went out. My father, who was much interested in his book, relighted the candle, stroked the cat, who was looking at him pathetically, he noticed, and continued his reading. A few minutes later, as the light became dim, he looked up just in time to see puss deliberately put out the candle with his paw, and then look appealingly at him. This second and unmistakeable hint was not disregarded and puss was given the petting he craved.

MARY DICKENS (CHARLES DICKENS'S DAUGHTER), *MY FATHER AS I RECALL HIM*

First published in the United States in 1992
by Chronicle Books

Conceived, edited and designed by Russell Ash & Bernard Higton
Copyright © 1992 by Russell Ash & Bernard Higton
Illustrations copyright © 1992 by Lesley Anne Ivory. Licensed by Copyrights

Printed in Hong Kong by Imago

ISBN 0-8118-0243-4

10 9 8 7 6 5 4 3 2 1

Chronicle Books
275 Fifth Street
San Francisco, California 94103

Text extracts from the following sources are reprinted with
the kind permission of the publishers and copyright holders stated.
Should any copyright holder have been inadvertently omitted
they should apply to the publishers, who will be pleased to credit them
in full in any subsequent editions: Colette, *Dialogues des Bêtes,*
reprinted by permission of Secker & Warburg Ltd;
Stephen Corbett, 'A Cat's Gratitude', reprinted by permission of the
author; Paul Gallico, *Honourable Cat,* reprinted by permission of
Souvenir Press Ltd and Random House, Inc.